Who God, The Father ("My Daddy") Is To Me From A to Z

For [the Spirit which] you have now received [is] not a spirit of slavery to put you once more in bondage to fear, but you have received the Spirit of adoption [the Spirit producing sonship] in [the bliss of] which we cry, Abba (Father)! Father! The Spirit Himself [thus] testifies together with our own spirit, [assuring us] that we are children of God.
(Romans 8:15-16, AMP)

Theresa Brooks Johnson

Who God, The Father ("My Daddy") Is To Me From A to Z
Copyright © 2004 by Theresa Brooks Johnson

Editor/Proofreader: Sister Lisa Moore

Front Cover Photography Copyright © By Morris Publishing

Author Photograph (Back Cover) By: ©The Picture People

ISBN: 0-9749187-0-9

Library of Congress Control Number: 2004092600

Printed in the United States by:
Morris Publishing
3212 East Highway 30
Kearney, NE 68847
1-800-650-7888
www.morrispublishing.com

Table of Contents

Acknowledgement

"In all your ways know, recognize, and acknowledge Him, and He will direct and make straight and plain your paths. (Proverbs 3:6, AMP)

To God, my Heavenly Father, Be All The Glory, All The Honor and All The Praise. You are truly worthy.

Father God, You are Alpha and Omega and Everything in between.

Because You are Infinite, there is and never will be a way to include all that You are in one book or volumes upon volumes of books. The Holy Spirit continues to reveal things about You to me daily, and for that I am grateful.

I love You, Abba ("Daddy").

Acknowledgements

To my husband, Larry – I love you (more than you'll ever know), but my Heavenly Father will always love you more. Receive all the love and plans that He has for you.

To my daughter, Lakisha and granddaughters, Cierra and Mykalah: I loved each of you before you entered the natural world. "Kisha" thanks for always asking about the progress of the book. "CC" & "KK" thanks for constantly reminding me of God's love when you say, "Grandma, God loves you." God, (Your Heavenly Daddy) loves all of you, and so do I. He has awesome plans for you. (Jeremiah 29:11 and Philippians 1:6)

To my Sisters in Christ: Carol Smith, Lisa Moore, Molly Britton, Jo-Ann Campbell, and Dawn Peterson. Thank you so much for your love, prayers, The Word, gifts, and support. I thank the Lord for bringing you in as "Aarons and Hurs" in the midst of some tough times. I dearly love each of you. I can only thank you, but know that God will reward your faithfulness.

A special thanks to The Moore Family for sowing seed into the vision before it ever went to print. Know that God will reward you openly. Also, thanks to Sister Lisa Moore for editing and proofreading this book. You are truly beloved of the Lord.

To every apostle, prophet, evangelist, pastor and teacher who have imparted Rhema Word into my spirit regarding the love of my Heavenly Father. A special thanks to Apostle Betty Peebles: you have "hugged" awesome truths from God's Word into my life, and I'll never be the same. Thanks to you all so much for being faithful vessels of God, Our Father.

TO GOD BE ALL THE GLORY!!!!

Dedication

This book is dedicated in memory of my earthly father, the late Rev. William H. Brooks, Sr., who entered eternity on June 3, 2003. Over the years, we had conversations about many things, especially his children. However, the conversations that I will treasure the most were those about our Heavenly Father and His goodness. This book is also dedicated in memory of my maternal grandmother, Mrs. Annie G. Murphy who entered eternity on May 24, 2003.

This book is dedicated to my entire, large family: my mother, Ms. Annie M. Brooks; stepmother, Ms. Willie M. Brooks; sisters and brothers: Linda, Anne, Brenda, William, Timothy, Benjamin, Renee, Reginald, Gerald, Charles, Roderick, and Carlos; stepsisters and stepbrother: Earnestine, Gloria and Donald. And all of my other family members (God knows you each by name.) Although you live in all parts of the world, I am thankful for Our Heavenly Father who is able to watch over and keep you in His care at the same time (He is Omnipresent). I truly love you. My prayer is that each of you will accept the full love of God, The Father so that you can receive all that He has for you (spirit, soul, and body). Know that He has awesome plans for each of you.

This book is also dedicated to every child of God – we are Family – all with the same "Daddy" (Father God).

Preface

**"Behold, what manner of love the Father hath bestowed upon us, that we should be called the sons of God..."
(1 John 3:1a)**

"For ye have not received the spirit of bondage again to fear; but ye have received the Spirit of adoption, whereby we cry, Abba, Father. The Spirit itself beareth witness with our spirit, that we are the children of God: (Romans 8:15-16)

1 John 3:1a & b in the Amplified Bible, reads as follows: "See what [an incredible] quality of love the Father has given (shown, bestowed on) us, that we should [be permitted to] be named *and* called *and* counted the children of God! And so we are!..." God's love has been presented as a gift upon us, that we should be called His sons (and daughters). His love will never change; however, the word *"should"* lets us know the choice of whether we accept His love to become His son (or daughter) lies with us.

In the 1950s or 1960s we grew up watching a show entitled "Father Knows Best." Although this was a television show with actors and actresses, we can be assured that our Heavenly Father is real and does know what is best for every one of His children. When we become His children (through His Son, Jesus), we are adopted into His family through the Spirit, and can now call Him Abba, Father.

According to Nelson's Illustrated Bible Dictionary, Abba is "an Aramaic word which corresponds to our "Daddy" or "Papa." (Nelson's Illustrated Bible Dictionary, 1986, page 2. Used by permission of Thomas Nelson, Inc.). When we hear the term "Daddy" or "Papa" we think of a provider and protector, love and so much more. Many individuals have a hard time seeing a loving God in the role of protector and provider because their earthly Dads have not done so. They also have a distorted view of God due to negative things they have heard about Him or their personal lack of knowledge about Him. I have heard terms such as "God will get you for that," and "God will have lightning strike you for that." Statements such as these portray God as as being mean and that He takes every opportunity to smack you with a stick for every wrong thing that you do. It also makes Him seem to be distant and unloving.

When an individual come to know God intimately, they will see that He is loving, does provide for His children and is very protective. Yes, He does correct, but it will always be done in love. His desire is to have a close relationship with each of His children where they can call Him Abba ("Daddy" or "Papa").

Through the Spirit of adoption, we are brought into a new and unique Family through and by the Lord Jesus Christ. We are now in a Family with the Father who knows everything, owns everything, and has all power. Everything we will ever need is in Him from A to Z. He knows our destiny, has the Master Plan for our lives, and has already been to our end. Isaiah 46:10 says of God: "Declaring the end from the beginning, and from ancient times the things that are not yet done, saying,

My counsel shall stand, and I will do all my pleasure:" Listen to The Father's words in Jeremiah 29:11 (AMP): "For I know the thoughts *and* plans that I have for you, says the Lord, thoughts *and* plans for welfare *and* peace and not for evil, to give you hope in your final outcome." What a Daddy!!!

There are only three simple chapters in this book, with the longest chapter (Chapter 2) reflecting on what the Word of God has to say about God, The Father. It is in the Word where we come to know The Father on an intimate and personal level. When God says something, we can believe it, stand on it, and trust Him totally. Isaiah 45:23 says "I have sworn by myself, the word is gone out of my mouth in righteousness, and shall not return…"

In Chapter 2, the attributes of God are listed under the alphabet in a certain series (A-Z), but not in particular alphabetical order for that particular page. I wrote as the Holy Spirit gave the information to me, and pray that you will accept them as listed. For example, under the As, "Alpha" has been listed first, and under the Cs, "Creator" has been listed first, therefore, they are not listed in alphabetical order on their particular pages.

An alphabetized glossary (which is in alphabetical order) has been placed at the very end of the book, beginning on page 69, to give more in-depth meaning and clearer understanding of some of the attributes of God, Our Father.

Be blessed as you read about Our Father ("Daddy').

Introduction

One day at the beginning of 2003 during early morning prayer as I kneeled to meet with the Lord, His presence was so, so sweet. On this particular morning there was something different in the atmosphere. I didn't want to ask for anything and no wrongs were brought to heart that I needed to confess.

I was led into a sweet adoration and time of worship to the Lord just for who He is. As the worship continued, I sensed the Holy Spirit revealing at a deeper level of Who God, the Father, has been, presently is, and will be to me in the future. John 16:13 says: "Howbeit when he, the Spirit of truth, is come, he will guide you into all truth: for he shall not speak of himself; but whatsoever he shall hear, *that* shall he speak: and he will show you things to come."

As I began to thank God for being the best Father any one could ever have, I wept and wept. His presence took me into new revelation knowledge of God not just as Father, but "Daddy." In my spirit I could hear the words "I love you" being spoken to me over and over again. It felt as if God had wrapped me up in His arms and was gently holding me.

My earthly dad was a good provider and firm disciplinarian, and for that I will always be grateful. I know that because he was a strong disciplinarian, instilled in me are morals and values that I still hold today. However, while growing up I do not recall him saying "I love you," giving hugs, or being affectionate. (I now realize that he showed affection as he had been taught, and loved as best he knew how to love). Later in life, as an adult, I did get to hear him say the words "I love you," which meant so much to me.

When I was eight years old my father and mother separated and later divorced. My dad had custody of us and I did not get to see my mother again until I was around 22 years old. As a young adult, I went looking for the love I thought I lacked and longed for in all the wrong places. It was only after Jesus was introduced to me did I begin to experience what true, pure and unconditional love was like. It was Jesus' unconditional love and devoted study of the Word of God that helped me begin the process of letting go of the bitterness I had allowed to enter my life regarding my childhood. I realized my spirit had been set free, but healing was still needed in my soul. Today, I love my parents dearly, and am grateful to God for both of them.

This special time of intimacy with the Lord, however, took me to another whole level in Him, and I will never be the same again. Because God is Alpha and Omega, and knows the end of all things, He revealed Himself as everything I needed in the past, presently need or will ever need Him to be in my life. On that morning, I began to worship Him for who He is to me from A to Z.

In April 2003, I was led to begin writing what I had

experienced that morning during worship. I asked the Holy Spirit to bring back to my memory what had been revealed to me, and He did so. As I was obedient to search the scriptures, I was even provided additional revelation knowledge that I had not received during that special time of worship.

I pray that as you read what the Word of God says about the Father, that His love will also take you to a whole new level in your life in Him. God is love and is so full of love, and desires to pour that love out onto His children. If you grew up without a father in your home, your father was in the home but distant, or your father is no longer here in the earth realm, allow The Heavenly Father's ("Daddy's") love to invade your heart, spirit and soul. You too, will no longer be the same.

By confessing verbally what the Word of God says about God, you will keep Him in or invite Him into every circumstance and situation that comes into your life. Also, by hearing what the Word of God says about Him will increase your faith. Romans 10:7 says "So then faith cometh by hearing, and hearing by the Word of God." So go ahead, put Him in remembrance of His Word (Isaiah 43:26) of who He says He is. Then stand still and behold His salvation (Exodus14: 13). Don't you want the love of God, Our Father ("Daddy")?

Confession of Salvation

Before we look at the three chapters within the book, I want to speak with you in the love of the Lord. If you have picked up this book, but has never established a personal relationship with the Lord Jesus Christ, (God's Only Begotten Son) I invite you to do so in order to receive the promises listed in His Word. I know this book is about knowing and receiving the love of God, the Father. However, please note John 14:6 (AMP): "Jesus said to him, I am the Way and the Truth and the Life; no one comes to the Father except by (through) Me." You must receive His Son (Jesus) before coming into an intimate relationship with God, The Father.

If you desire that relationship, please bow your head and use your voice (which is a life force) and say aloud: LORD JESUS, COME INTO MY LIFE. I CONFESS WITH MY MOUTH THE LORD JESUS AND BE- LIEVE IN MY HEART THAT GOD RAISED HIM

FROM THE DEAD." Romans 10:9-10 says "That if thou shalt confess with thy mouth the Lord Jesus, and shalt believe in thine heart that God hath raised Him from the dead, thou shalt be saved. For with the heart man believeth unto righteousness; and with the mouth confession is made unto salvation."

When you confessed Romans 10:9-10 you are now saved (born again), a new creature in Christ Jesus, and an heir to the promises in God's Word. The angels are rejoicing in Heaven. To God Be All The Glory!!!

I now encourage you to pray, read and confess the Word of God daily. Also, live holy and connect with a body of believers where the uncompromised Word of God is being taught, whereby you may continue to grow and draw closer to the Lord. By reading the Word of God and obeying it; being led by the Holy Spirit; and fellowshipping with other believers, you'll get to know God, The Father ("Daddy") more intimately.

Reconnecting with God After Broken Fellowship

Some of you reading this book once confessed Jesus as the Lord, but have been out of fellowship with Him due to sin. The devil, other people, and even *yourself*, have convinced you that God no longer loves you and there is no hope for you. This is a lie!!! Our Heavenly Father never stopped loving you and His arms are always open and ready to welcome you back into fellowship with Him. 1 John 1:9 (AMP) says: "If we [freely] admit that we have sinned *and* confess our sins, He is faithful and just (true to His own nature and promises) and will forgive our sins [dismiss our lawlessness] and [continuously] cleanse us from all unrighteousness [everything not in conformity to His will in purpose, thought and action]."

God is just waiting to hear you call to Him and ask for forgiveness so that He can cleanse you and set you back in line with His purpose for your life that will bring glory and honor unto Him.

If you desire to get back into fellowship with your Heavenly Father, verbally say (aloud) the following: "FATHER GOD, IN THE NAME OF THE LORD JESUS, I COME BEFORE YOU CONFESSING THAT I HAVE SINNED AGAINST YOU (STATE THE SIN). FATHER, I ASK FOR YOUR FORGIVENESS AND YOUR CLEANSING FROM MY SIN. BECAUSE I KNOW THAT YOU ARE A GOD WHO WILL NOT LIE, I RECEIVE YOUR FORGIVENESS AND CLEANSING. I KNOW THAT I AM NOW BACK IN FELLOWSHIP WITH YOU. THANK YOU FATHER. IN THE NAME OF THE LORD JESUS. SO BE IT. AMEN.

You are now back in fellowship with your Heavenly Father. Go boldly before His throne daily to meet with Him to allow Him to love on you as you love on Him. To God Be All The Glory!!!

Chapter 1

Only God, The Father Can Fill the Vacuum Within Us

Chapter 1

Only God, The Father Can Fill The Vacuum Within Us

As I was working on this book, I took a break to watch a segment that was airing on television. As a matter of fact, it only had 10 minutes left when I cut the set on. The show was about children and their fathers who had never had close relationships with each other. Some of the fathers and children were bitter and some were teary. Most of the children were teens and adults. There were professionals who were trying their best to give advice on what had been missing and why there was such emptiness in each relationship and each individual.

I knew that God Almighty had allowed me to see this segment "for such a time as this" and I began to groan in my spirit. I also knew at that time that this book was in the divine will of God. As I looked at the set, I said, "if you only had the love of my Father, the love of my Daddy." One scripture that came to mind was Psalm 27:10, which was so consoling to me during the healing process of the pain of my childhood. Psalm 27:10 says "When my father and my mother forsake me, then the LORD will take me up." With God as Our Father, the emptiness is gone because He fills the void that no one else can fill.

During 2003, I heard Apostle Betty Peebles (Senior Pastor, Jericho City of Praise in Landover, Maryland) speak about the vacuum within us during a message. The message was such a blessing and personal revelation knowledge was imparted into me at that time. Part of what I had tried to understand with my finite mind was answered that morning, and I will always be grateful to God for using her to minister an "on-time" Word from the Lord.

In the message, Apostle Betty stated that we come

with a vacuum within us that no one else can fill but God Himself. He designed it that way. No earthly father, mother, brother, sister, mate, friend, sex, drugs, hobbies, houses, cars, etc can fill it. Let's be clear, there is nothing wrong with having close relationships (when they are in accordance with the Word of God) or material possessions (when obtained through the blessings of God). As a matter of fact God wants us to have both, but they can not, and never will be able to fill the vacuum reserved for God and God alone.

If you have been one who did not have a godly example to learn what the Heavenly Father was like, then get to know The Father now (through the Word of God). It is not too late – He is waiting for you to call on Him as "Abba" or "Daddy." Jeremiah 33:3 says "Call unto me, and I will answer thee, and show thee great and mighty things, which thou knowest not." Take note that the Lord says He will not just answer you, but will show you, *yes you*, great and mighty things. Hallelujah!!! Great and mighty are two of the attributes He revealed Himself to be to me (look at the Gs and Ms). I am so excited and in great expectation of Who God will reveal Himself to you as you open up His Word. To God Be All The Glory!!!!

Chapter 2

Attributes of God, The Father ("Daddy")
(From the Word of God – A to Z)

The term "My Daddy" listed throughout Chapter 2 refers to God, My Heavenly Father.

My Daddy is

Alpha

Almighty

Awesome

Revelation 1:8: I am *Alpha* and Omega, the beginning and the ending, saith the Lord, which is, and which was, and which is to come, the *Almighty*.

Psalm 33:8: Let all the earth fear the LORD: let all the inhabitants of the world stand in *awe* of him.

Confession: My Daddy is Alpha – The Beginning. He knew my beginning before I was ever born. He is Almighty, and I stand in awe of Him. My Heavenly Father is an awesome God.

My Daddy is a

Buckler

Psalm 18:30: *As for* God, his way *is* perfect: the word of the LORD is tried: he *is* a **buckler** to all those that trust in him.

Proverbs 2:7: He layeth up sound wisdom for the righteous: *he is* a **buckler** to them that walk uprightly.

Confession: My Daddy is my buckler – this means that He is my shield and my protector. Because I trust Him and walk upright He will continue to be my buckler.

My Daddy (is)

Creator (Elohim)

A Consuming Fire

Chastens Me

Isaiah 40:28: Hast thou not known? hast thou not heard, that the everlasting God, the LORD, the *Creator* of the ends of the earth, fainteth not, neither is weary? there is no searching of his understanding.

Hebrews 12:29: For our God *is **a consuming fire***.

Hebrews 12:6: For whom the Lord loveth he *chasteneth,* and scourgeth every son whom he receiveth.

Confession: My Daddy is my Creator; *The Creator*. He is a consuming fire that burns away those things in my life that do not bring Him glory. My Heavenly Father corrects me because he loves me.

My Daddy is

A Covenant-Keeper

Daniel 9:4: And I prayed unto the LORD my God, and made my confession, and said, O Lord, the great and dreadful God, *keeping the covenant* and mercy to them that love him, and to them that keep his commandments;

Deuteronomy 7:9 (AMP): Know, recognize, *and* understand therefore that the Lord your God, He is God, the faithful God, *Who keeps covenant* and steadfast love *and* mercy with those who love Him and keep His commandments, to a thousand generations,

Judges 2:1: And an angel of the LORD came up from Gilgal to Bochim, and said, I made you to go up out of Egypt, and have brought you into the land which I sware unto your fathers; and I said, *I will never break my covenant with you.*

Confession: My Daddy always keeps His covenant (contract or agreement) with me and my seed. As we love Him and keep His commandments He will continue to keep His covenant with us, to a thousand generations. Hallelujah!!! My Daddy will never break His covenant with me.

My Daddy (is)

Daily Loads me with Benefits

My Deliverer

Psalm 68:19: Blessed *be* the Lord, *who **daily loadeth us with benefits**, even* the God of our salvation. Selah.

Psalm 144:2 (AMP): My Steadfast Love and my Fortress, my High Tower and my ***Deliverer***, my Shield and He in Whom I trust *and* take refuge, Who subdues my people under me.

Confession: My Daddy daily supplies me abundantly with benefits. Some of those benefits are healing, health, protection, and peace. Thank You, Father God, for your daily benefits unto me. God is my deliverer.

My Daddy is

El Elyon (The Most High God)

Everlasting

El Roi (The God Who Sees)

Genesis 14:22: And Abram said to the king of Sodom, I have lift up mine hand unto the LORD, *the most high God,* the possessor of heaven and earth,

Isaiah 9:6: For unto us a child is born, unto us a son is given: and the government shall be upon his shoulder: and his name shall be called Wonderful, Counsellor, The mighty God, The *everlasting* Father, The Prince of Peace.

Genesis 16: 13: And she called the name of the LORD that spake unto her, ***Thou God seest me***: for she said, Have I also here looked after him that seeth me?

Confession: My Daddy is El Elyon, the Most High God, and I know that there is no one higher than He. He is the everlasting Father, the Prince of Peace. My Heavenly Father sees everything that goes on in my life; nothing about me or done to me escapes His eye.

My Daddy is

Faithful

1 Corinthians 1:9: God *is faithful,* by whom ye were called unto the fellowship of his Son Jesus Christ our Lord.

1 Thessalonians 5:24: *Faithful is* he that calleth you, who also will do *it.*

Confession: My Daddy is faithful. He has called me and He is faithful; He will do it. Hallelujah!!!

My Daddy is

God

Good

Isaiah 46:9: Remember the former things of old: for I am *God*, and there is none else; I am *God*, and there is none like me,

Psalm 100:5: For the LORD *is* ***good***; his mercy *is* everlasting; and his truth *endureth* to all generations.

(***Author's Note***: There were approximately 50 definitions in the dictionary for the word "good." I encourage you to take the time to look up the word "good" in your dictionary. It will bless you.)

Confession: My Daddy is God, and there is none else, no, there is none like Him. My Heavenly Father is a good God; He is excellent and genuine, not a counterfeit.

My Daddy is

A Giver

John 3:16: For God so loved the world, that He *gave* his only begotten Son, that whosoever believeth in him should not perish, but have everlasting life.

Deuteronomy 8:18 (AMP): But you shall [earnestly] remember the Lord your God, for it is He Who *gives* you power to get wealth, that He may establish His covenant which He swore to your fathers, as it is this day.

Confession: My Daddy is a giver. Because of His gift of His Son, Jesus I will not perish and I have everlasting life. He gives me power to get wealth so that His covenant is established. As I am given the power to get wealth I will be able to give so that His kingdom can be furthered and I can bless others.

My Daddy is

Great

My Guide

Jeremiah 10:6: Forasmuch as there is none like unto thee, O LORD; thou art ***great***, and thy name is great in might.

Psalm 32:8: I will instruct thee and teach thee in the way which thou shalt go: I will ***guide*** thee with mine eye.

Confession: My Daddy is great and His name is great. He guides me with His eye.

My Daddy (is)

Holy

Hastens to Perform His Word

My Husband

Psalm 99:9: Exalt the LORD our God, and worship at his holy hill; for the LORD our God *is **holy.***

Jeremiah 1:12: Then said the LORD unto me, Thou hast well seen: for I will ***hasten my word to perform it***.

Isaiah 54:5: For thy Maker is thine ***husband***; the LORD of hosts is his name; and thy Redeemer the Holy One of Israel; The God of the whole earth shall he be called.

Confession: My Heavenly Father is holy. My Daddy is swift in seeing that His Word is performed on my behalf. Glory!!! As my Maker, my Heavenly Father is also my Husband (my first love).

My Daddy is

My Healer
(Jehovah Rapha)

Exodus 15:26 (AMP): Saying, If you will diligently hearken to the voice of the Lord your God and will do what is right in His sight, and will listen to *and* obey His commandments and keep all His statues, I will put none of the diseases upon you which I brought upon the Egyptians, for ***I am the Lord Who heals you.***

Psalm 103:3 (AMP): Who forgives [every one of] all your iniquities, ***Who heals*** [each one of] all your diseases,

Confession: My Heavenly Father is my healer. He forgives all my iniquities and has healed all of my diseases. By the stripes of His Son, Jesus I am already healed.

My Daddy (is)

"I AM"

Infinite

Inhabits the Praises of His People

Exodus 3:14: And God said unto Moses, *I AM THAT I AM*: and he said, Thus shalt thou say unto the children of Israel, *I AM* hath sent me unto you.

Psalm 147:5 (AMP): Great is our Lord and of great power; *His understanding is inexhaustible and boundless*.

Psalm 22:3: But thou *art* holy, O *thou* that *inhabitest the praises* of Israel.

Confession: My Daddy is "I AM." I am finite, but my Heavenly Father is Infinite – unlimited and having no bounds. When I worship Him, He lives in or dwells in my praise. Hallelujah!!!

My Daddy is

Jealous

Exodus 34:14 (AMP): For you shall worship no other god; for the Lord, Whose name is *Jealous*, is a *jealous* (impassioned) God.

Confession: My Daddy is a jealous God. Therefore, I worship no other gods. His name is Jealous.

My Daddy is

Just

Joy

Revelation 16:7 (AMP): And [from] the altar I heard [the] cry, Yes, Lord God the Omnipotent, Your judgments (sentences, decisions) are true *and just* and righteous!

Zephaniah 3:17: The LORD thy God in the midst of thee is mighty; he will save, he will rejoice over thee with *joy*; he will rest in his love, he will *joy* over thee with singing.

Nehemiah 8:10: Then he said unto them, Go your way, eat the fat, and drink the sweet, and send portions unto them for whom nothing is prepared: for *this* day *is* holy unto our Lord: neither be ye sorry; for the *joy* of the LORD is your strength.

Confession: My Heavenly Father is just with His judgments (sentences and decisions). He rejoices over me with joy and with singing. Hallelujah!!! The joy of my Daddy gives me strength.

My Daddy is

Jehovah
(The God Who Reveals Himself)

Genesis 22:14: And Abraham called the name of that place *Jehovahjireh*: as it is said to this day, In the mount of the LORD it shall be seen.
(Jehovah Jireh means "The LORD Will Provide")

Exodus 17:15: And Moses built an altar, and called the name of it *Jehovahnissi*:
(Jehovah Nissi means "The LORD is My Banner")

Judges 6:24: Then Gideon built an altar there unto the LORD, and called it *Jehovahshalom*: unto this day it *is* yet in Ophrah of the Abiezrites.
(Jehovah Shalom means "The LORD is Peace")

Ezekiel 48:35: It was round about eighteen thousand measures: and the name of the city from that day shall be, *The LORD is there.*
(Jehovah Shammah means "The LORD is there")

Confession: My Daddy is Jehovah who reveals Himself to me as my provider, banner, peace and healer. He is always there for me.

My Daddy is

Kind

My Keeper

Psalm 117:2: For his merciful *kindness* is great toward us: and the truth of the LORD *endureth* for ever. Praise ye the LORD.

Psalm 121:5: *The LORD is thy keeper*: the LORD *is* thy shade upon thy right hand.

Confession: My Daddy's merciful kindness is great toward me, and His truth endureth forever. The Lord is my keeper, which means He guards, maintains and watches over me. He keeps me by preserving me because I am valuable to Him.

My Daddy is

Love

Longsuffering

The Lifter of My Head

John 3:16 (AMP): For God so greatly *loved* and dearly prized the world that He [even] gave up His only begotten (unique) Son, so that whoever believes in (trusts in, clings to, relies on) Him shall not perish (come to destruction, be lost) but have eternal (everlasting) life.

Numbers 14:18: The LORD *is longsuffering,* and of great mercy, forgiving iniquity and transgression, and by no means clearing *the guilty,* visiting the iniquity of the fathers upon the children unto the third and fourth *generation.*

Psalm 3:3: But thou, O LORD, *art* a shield for me; my glory, and *the lifter up of mine head.*

Confession: My Daddy loves me. He is longsuffering, great in mercy, and forgives my iniquities and transgressions. When circumstances try to make me lower my head, My Heavenly Father lifts my head.

My Daddy is

Merciful

Mighty

Deuteronomy 4:31: (For the LORD thy God *is* a *merciful* God;) he will not forsake thee, neither destroy thee, nor forget the covenant of thy fathers which he sware unto them.

Psalm 24:8: Who *is* this King of Glory? The LORD strong and *mighty*, the LORD *mighty* in battle.

Jeremiah 32:18 (AMP): You Who show loving-kindness to thousands but recompense the iniquity of the fathers into the bosoms of their children after them. The great, the *mighty* God; the Lord of hosts is His name -

Confession: My Daddy is merciful, he will not forsake me, destroy me or forget the covenant he has made unto me. He is mighty in battle on my behalf. The Lord of hosts is His name.

My Daddy is

Near

My Need Supplier

Psalm 119:151 (AMP): You are *near*, O Lord [nearer to me than my foes], and all Your commandments are truth.

Philippians 4:19 (AMP): And my God will liberally *supply (fill to the full) your every need* according to His riches in glory in Christ Jesus.

Confession: My Daddy is near to me. He supplies all my need according to His riches in glory in Christ Jesus.

My Daddy is

Omniscient

Omnipresent

Isaiah 40: 13-14: Who hath directed the Spirit of the LORD, or being his counsellor hath taught him? With whom took he counsel and who instructed him, and taught him in the path of judgement, and taught him knowledge, and showed to him the way of understanding? ***(God is Omniscient. He is All Knowing. No one has to and no one can direct, instruct, teach or counsel Him regarding knowledge.)***

Psalm 139: 7-10: Whither shall I go from thy spirit? or whither shall I flee from thy presence? If I ascend up into heaven, thou *art* there: if I make my bed in hell, behold, thou *art there. If* I take the wings of the morning, *and* dwell in the uttermost parts of the sea; Even there shall thy hand lead me, and thy right hand shall hold me. ***(God is Omnipresent. He is everywhere at all times. There is no where I can go that He is not there.)***

Confession: (Confess the statements listed in bold following the listed scriptures.)

My Daddy is

Omnipotent

Omega

Revelation 19:6: And I heard as it were the voice of a great multitude, and as the voice of many waters, and as the voice of mighty thunderings, saying, Alleluia: for the Lord God *omnipotent* reigneth.

Revelation 22:13: I am Alpha and *Omega*, the beginning and the end, the first and the last.

Isaiah 46:10: Declaring the *end* from the beginning, and from ancient times the things that are not yet done, saying, My counsel shall stand, and I will do all my pleasure.

Confession: My Heavenly Father is Omnipotent – He is All Powerful. My Daddy is Omega, which means He is the end and knows the end of all things. He knows my end from the beginning.

My Daddy is

Patient

Peace

Romans 15:5: Now the God of *patience* and consolation grant you to be likeminded one toward another according to Christ Jesus:

Romans 15:33 (AMP): May [our] *peace*-giving God be with you all! Amen (so be it).

Confession: My Daddy is patient with me; therefore, I am to also be patient with others. God is peace to me. He is a peace-giving God.

My Daddy

Has Quickened Me

Quickens My Mortal Body

Ephesians 2:1, 5: And *you hath he quickened*, who were dead in trespasses and sins: Even when we were dead in sins, *hath quickened us* together with Christ, (by grace ye are saved;)

Romans 8:11: But if the Spirit of him that raised up Jesus from the dead dwell in you, he that raised up Christ from the dead shall also *quicken your mortal bodies* by his Spirit that dwelleth in you.

Confession: When my Daddy raised Jesus from the dead, He also raised me up even when I was dead in trespasses and sins. My Heavenly Father, who raised Jesus from the dead also quickens my mortal body by His Spirit that dwelleth in me.

My Daddy is

Righteous

The Rewarder

Jeremiah 9:24: But let him that glorieth glory in this, that he understandeth and knoweth me, that I am the LORD which exercise lovingkindness, judgment, and *righteousness*, in the earth: for in these things I delight, saith the LORD.

Philippians 3:9: And be found in him, not having mine own righteousness, which is of the law, but that which is through the faith of Christ, the *righteousness* which is of God by faith.

Hebrews 11:6 (AMP): But without faith it is impossible to please *and* be satisfactory to Him. For whoever would come near to God must [necessarily] believe that God exists and that He is the *rewarder* of those who earnestly *and* diligently seek Him [out].

Confession: My Daddy is Righteous, and because of His Son, Jesus I am righteous also. My Heavenly Father rewards me when I earnestly and diligently seek Him.

My Daddy is

My Redeemer

My Refuge

Job 19:25: For I know *that* my **redeemer** liveth, and *that* he shall stand at the latter *day* upon the earth:

Psalm 31:5: Into thine hand I commit my spirit: thou hast **redeemed** me, O LORD God of truth.

Ephesians 1:7: In whom we have **redemption** through his blood, the forgiveness of sins, according to the riches of his grace;

Psalm 91:2: I will say of the LORD, He is my **refuge**…

Confession: My Heavenly Father is my redeemer. Through the redemption of the blood of Jesus Christ I also have the forgiveness of sins, according to the riches of His grace. My Daddy is my refuge, which means He is my shelter and protection from danger and trouble.

My Daddy is

My Sanctification

My Shield

My Shepherd

Jude (verse 1): Jude, the servant of Jesus Christ, and brother of James, to them that are *sanctified* by God the Father, and preserved in Jesus Christ, called:

Psalm 33:20 (AMP): Our inner selves wait [earnestly] for the Lord; He is our Help and our *Shield*.

Psalm 23: 1 (AMP): The LORD is my *Shepherd* [to feed, guide, and shield me], I shall not lack.

Confession: My Daddy has sanctified (preserved, separated and set apart) me. He has also called me. He is my shield. My Heavenly Father is my Shepherd – He feeds me, guides me and shields me. I shall not lack anything. Glory!!!

My Daddy is

A Tower

Truth

Proverbs 18:10: The name of the LORD *is* a strong *tower*: the righteous runneth into it, and is safe.

Psalm 61:3 (AMP): For You have been a shelter *and* a refuge for me, a strong *tower* against the adversary.

Deuteronomy 32:4: *He is* the Rock, his work *is* perfect: for all his ways *are* judgement: a God of *truth* and without iniquity, just and right *is* he.

Confession: My Daddy is a strong tower. I am one of the righteous; therefore, I am able to run into that strong tower, and there I am safe. My Heavenly Father is a shelter and a refuge for me against my enemy. He is truth, He cannot lie.

My Daddy is

Unchanging

Malachi 3:6: For I am the LORD, *I change not*; therefore ye sons of Jacob are not consumed.

Hebrews 1:12 (AMP): Like a mantle [thrown about one's self] You will roll them up, and they will be changed *and* replaced by others. But *You remain the same,* and Your years will never end *no*r come to failure.

Confession: My Daddy changes not; therefore, I am not consumed. I never have to be concerned about my Heavenly Father being one way today, and another way tomorrow because He always remains the same.

My Daddy is

A Very Present Help in Trouble

Very Great

Valiant in His Right Hand

Psalm 46:1: God is our refuge and strength, *a very present help in trouble*.

Psalm 104:1: Bless the LORD, O my soul. O LORD my God, thou art *very great*; thou art clothed with honour and majesty.

Psalm 118:16: The right hand of the LORD is exalted: *the right hand of the LORD doeth valiantly*.

Confession: My Daddy is a very present help in trouble. Glory to God!!!   My Heavenly Father is not just a great God, but a *very* great God. He is brave and courageous in His right hand.

My Daddy's /My Daddy

Way is Perfect

Shall Wipe Away All Tears

Is Worthy

Psalm 18:30: *As for* God, his ***way is perfect***: the word of the LORD is tried: he *is* a buckler to all those that trust in him.

Revelation 21:4: And God ***shall wipe away all tears*** from their eyes; and there shall be no more death, neither sorrow, nor crying, neither shall there be any more pain: for the former things are passed away.

Psalm 18:3: I will call upon the LORD, ***who is worthy*** to be praised…

Confession: My Daddy's way is perfect. Revelation 21:4 tells me that one day He shall wipe away all tears from my eyes. My Heavenly Father is worthy, He is truly worthy of all the praise!!!

My Daddy is

The X-rayer of my Heart

1 Samuel 16:7: But the LORD said unto Samuel, Look not on his countenance, or on the height of his stature; because I have refused him: for *the LORD seeth* not as man seeth; for man looketh on the outward appearance, but *the LORD looketh on the heart*.

Confession: My Daddy knows the very thoughts and intents of my heart, and sees what no one else is able to see. Man looks at my outward appearance, but God is able to see my heart.

My Daddy says

"Yes" to His Promises in Christ Jesus

2 Corinthians 1:20 (AMP): For as many as *are the promises of God, they all find their Yes [answer] in Him [Christ].* For this reason we also utter the Amen (so be it) to God through Him [in His Person and by His agency] to the glory of God.

Confession: My Daddy's answer is "yes" to His promises in Christ Jesus. For this reason I utter Amen (so be it) to God through Jesus to the glory of God.

My Daddy is

Zealous

2 Kings 19:31: For out of Jerusalem shall go forth a remnant, and they that escape out of mount Zion: the *zeal* of the LORD *of hosts* shall do this.

Confession: My Daddy is zealous. His enthusiastic diligence for me let's me know that I am number one on His agenda.

Chapter 3

Postscript:
God is Faithful and True to His Word

Chapter 3

Postscript:
God is Faithful and True to His Word

So much has transpired since the writing of this book began in early 2003. I initially assumed that after Chapter 2 was written, nothing more needed to be added. However, because of major events that have occurred in my life since it began, I was led by the Holy Spirit to give testimony of God's faithfulness and His goodness to me. Some of what had been written in the previous pages of Who God had revealed Himself to be to me, was experienced in my life during the late Spring and Summer of 2003, and into 2004.

My 96 year-old maternal grandmother and 75 year-old father are no longer here with us in the earth realm because they entered eternity on May 24, 2003 (grandmother) and June 3, 2003 (father). During the calls from family to let us know, making the trips to Birmingham, Alabama for the services, and afterwards, God has revealed Himself as Jehovah Shalom. God's peace has kept and sustained me. He has never left me or forsaken me during this time, and I am so thankful to Him for that.

On Saturday, August 23, 2003, another driver ran a red light and ran into the right side of my car. I am so thankful that God is my shield and protector, and had given His angels charge over me to keep me on that day. To God Be All The Glory because the other driver and myself both walked away from the accident with no physical hurt or harm to either of us. Although the insurance company deemed my car a total loss, I am still here because of the mercies and grace of God. God has provided another vehicle (debt free) because He is Jehovah Jireh, my Provider. Although the car is not a new one, I am still thankful. God has given a vision of a new car and He keeps the vision before my eyes. My "Daddy" continues to supply all my need according to His riches in glory in Christ Jesus (Philippians 4:19).

During the week of October 19, 2003, while going through papers, I came across two letters (the only ones) that my dad had written to me since I left home in 1974. One of the letter's papers had turned yellow, but the words on them were such a blessing to me. Although my dad only received a seventh grade education, and did not like to write because of that, I could feel the genuine love in these letters. Over the years we did not agree on many issues, but I am thankful that the Lord enabled me to respect and honor him. My earthly father is no longer here, but there is a comfort in knowing that my Heavenly Father will always be here. Every day when I pick up the Word of God I am receiving a personal love letter from my "Heavenly Daddy" and for that I am very grateful.

In 2004, other challenges have presented themselves, but God continues to be a strong tower that I run to constantly and there I am safe. While working on this project (God's work), the computer somehow rearranged the document and I had to retype the entire book, but God's peace remained upon me and in me. As I retyped, the Lord just used that time to refill me with His Word and with His love. There are also issues my family is currently facing, but God has already been to the end and we are victorious. No matter what circumstances come my way, I know that my Heavenly Father ("Daddy") continues to be all that I need and will ever need Him to be from A to Z. In Christ Jesus, I am always triumphant and more than a conqueror. The Holy Spirit continues to lead and guide me to the expected end that God has for me. Since The Father, Son and Holy Spirit are One; I can not lose, but will always be victorious.

To God Be All The Glory!!!!

Glossary

<u>Glossary</u>

Almighty –…having absolute power over all…; relatively unlimited in power; great in magnitude or seriousness…

Alpha – …something that is first: **BEGINNING**…

(Awe)some – …an emotion variously combining dread, veneration, and wonder that is inspired by authority or by the sacred or sublime…

Benefit – …an act of kindness: **BENEFACTION**; something that promotes well-being: **ADVANTAGE**; useful aid: **HELP**…

Boundless – having no boundaries: **VAST**

Buckler – …one that shields and protects

Change – …to make different in some particular: **ALTER**;…to make radically different: **TRANS-FORM**…; to give a different position, course, or direction to…

All definitions on this page are used "By permission. From **Merriam-Webster's Online Dictionary** © 2004 by Merriam-Webster, Incorporated (www. Merriam-Webster.com)."

Chasten – …to prune (as a work or style of art) of excess, pretense, or falsity: **REFINE**; to cause to be more humble or restrained: **SUBDUE**…

Consume – …to do away with completely: **DESTROY**…

Creator – …one that creates usually by bringing something new or original into being; *especially capitalized*: **GOD**

Daily – occurring, made or acted upon every day;…of or providing for every day…

El Elyon – "a Hebrew name for God. Translated into English, it means "God Most High"….(Nelson's Illustrated Bible Dictionary© 1986 by Thomas Nelson Publishers, pg 328. Used by permission of Thomas Nelson, Inc.)

Everlasting – …lasting or enduring through all time: **ETERNAL**; continuing long or indefinitely…

Faithful – …steadfast in affection or allegiance: **LOYAL**…

Give – …to make a present of;…to put into the possession of another for his use…

God – "the creator and sustainer of the universe who has provided humankind with a revelation of Himself through the natural world and through His Son, Jesus Christ." (Nelson's Illustrated Bible Dictionary © 1986 by Thomas Nelson Publishers, pg. 425. Used by permission of Thomas Nelson, Inc.)

Great – …notably large in size: **HUGE**;…remarkable in magnitude, degree or effectiveness…

Guide – …to direct, supervise or influence usually to a particular end…

Hasten – …to urge on;…**ACCELERATE**…

Help – to give assistance or support to;…to make more pleasant or bearable: **IMPROVE, RELIEVE**;… **RESCUE, SAVE**…

Holy – moral and ethical wholeness or perfection; freedom from moral evil. (Nelson's Illustrated Bible Dictionary © 1986 by Thomas Nelson Publishers, page 485. Used by permission of Thomas Nelson, Inc.)

"I Am" – "…signals the truth that nothing else defines who God is but God Himself. What He says and does is who He is…" (Nelson's Illustrated Bible Dictionary © 1986 by Thomas Nelson Publishers, page 427. Used by permission of Thomas Nelson, Inc.)

Inhabit – …to occupy as a place of settled residence or habitat; live in…

Infinite – …extending indefinitely: **ENDLESS**…; **INEXHAUSTIBLE**…

Joy – …the emotion evoked by well-being success, or good fortune or by the prospect of possessing what one desires: **DELIGHT**…

Just – …acting or being in conformity with what is morally upright or good: **RIGHTEOUS…**

Kind – …**AFFECTIONATE, LOVING**;…of a forbearing nature: **GENTLE**…

Load – …to supply in abundance or excess: **HEAP, PACK**…

Longsuffering – "a word in the KJV and NKJV that refers primarily to God's patient endurance of the wickedness of the sinful (Ex. 34:6). The purpose of God's longsuffering is to lead people to repentance (Rom 2:4; 2 Pet 3:9, 15)... (Nelson's Illustrated Bible Dictionary © 1986 by Thomas Nelson Publishers, page 652. Used by permission of Thomas Nelson, Inc.)

Love – ...strong affection for another arising out of kinship or personal ties...; warm attachment, enthusiasm, or devotion...

Loyal – ...unswerving in allegiance...

Mercy – ...A compassion or forbearance shown especially to an offender or to one subject to one's power...

Mighty – ...possessing might: **POWERFUL**;...great or imposing in size or extent: **EXTRAORDINARY**

Mortal – ...subject to death; ...**HUMAN**...

Near – at, within, or to a short distance or time…; in a close or intimate manner: **CLOSELY**…

Need - …a physiological or psychological requirement for the well being of an organism; a condition requiring supply or relief…

Omega - …**LAST, ENDING**…

Omnipotent – …having virtually unlimited authority or influence…

Omnipresent – …present in all places at all times

Omniscient - having infinite awareness, understanding, and insight; possessed of universal or complete knowledge…

Patient – steadfast despite opposition, difficulty, or adversity…

Peace – a state of tranquility or quiet…; freedom from disquieting or oppressive thoughts or emotions…

Perfect – …being entirely without any fault or defect: **FLAWLESS**…; lacking in no essential detail: **COMPLETE**…

Present - …now existing or in progress; being in view or at hand…; **INSTANT, IMMEDIATE**

Promise – …a declaration that one will do or refrain from doing something specified…

Quicken – to make alive: **REVIVE**…

Redeem – to buy back: **REPURCHASE**…to release from blame or debt: **CLEAR**…

Refuge – shelter or protection from danger or distress, a place that provides shelter or protection…

Reward – …something that is given in return for good or evil done or received especially that is offered or given for some service or attainment…

Righteous – …morally right or justifiable…

Sanctify – …to set apart to a sacred purpose… **CONSECRATE**; to free from sin: **PURIFY**…

Shield – …one that protects or defends: **DEFENSE**…

Supply – …to provide for: **SATISFY**…; to make available for use: **PROVIDE**…

Trouble – to agitate mentally or spiritually: **WORRY**: **DISTURB**…

Truth – …**FIDELITY, CONSTANCY**, sincerity in action, character, and utterance…

Unlimited – …lacking any controls: **UNRE-STRICTED; BOUNDLESS, INFINITE**; not bounded by exceptions: **UNDEFINED**…

Valiant – …possessing or acting with bravery or boldness: **COURAGEOUS**…

Very – …to a high degree: **EXCEEDINGLY**…

Yes – …use as a function word to express assent or agreement...

Zeal – …eagerness and ardent interest in pursuit of something: **FERVOR**...

Bibliography

Merriam-Webster's Online Dictionary © 2004 by Merriam-Webster, Incorporated (www.Merriam-Webster.com).

Nelson's Illustrated Bible Dictionary. Copyright © 1986 by Thomas Nelson Publishers. Published in Nashville, Tennessee by Thomas Nelson, Inc.

About the Author

Theresa Brooks Johnson was naturally born to her parents, William and Annie Mae Brooks in 1955 in Birmingham, Alabama. She was spiritually born again and adopted into the Family of God in February 1980, while stationed in the United States Air Force at Andrews AFB, Maryland. Theresa was baptized and filled with the Holy Spirit (with the evidence of speaking in other tongues) in January 1982. Although Jesus became her Savior in 1980, while she was a pregnant, unwed mother, He did not become her Lord until 1997. The Holy Spirit revealed to her that Jesus was more than Savior, He is also The Lord. In 1997, Theresa acknowledged Him as The Lord and The Lord (Master and Ruler) of her life.

The gift The Lord has placed within her in the Body of Christ is one that exhorts (encourages), edifies (stirs/builds up) and comforts (cheers up) others as led by the Holy Spirit. The passion and prayers she have for unbelievers is to see them totally surrender their hearts and lives to Jesus.

Theresa currently lives in Clinton, Maryland and is married to Larry Johnson. They are the parents of one daughter, Lakisha, and grandparents of two granddaughters, Cierra (age 6) and Mykalah (age 3). They are members of Evangel Assembly of God, Camp Springs, Maryland.

The Gift
(Baptism in the Holy Spirit or Holy Ghost)

If ye then, being evil, know how to give good gifts unto your children: how much more shall your heavenly Father give the Holy Spirit to them that ask him? (Luke 11:13)

Since you are a reborn, saved child of God, you can *ask* The Father to fill you with the Holy Spirit (with the evidence of speaking in other tongues). The Holy Spirit is a Gift unto us, God's sons and daughters. John 14:26 says "But the Comforter, *which is* the Holy Ghost, whom the Father will send in my name, he shall teach you all things, and bring all things to your remembrance, whatsoever I have said unto you." In these last days, we need the power of The Holy Spirit to guide, teach and lead us so that we can fulfill all that God wants to do through us for His glory. It is through the Holy Spirit that we hear what Our Heavenly Father is saying.

If you desire to be filled with the Holy Spirit, ask the Father through these words: 'FATHER, IN THE NAME OF THE LORD JESUS, I AM ASKING YOU TO FILL ME WITH THE HOLY SPIRIT. I KNOW THAT AS I YIELD MY OWN VOICE TO YOU, YOU WILL GIVE ME THE UTTERANCE TO SPEAK IN OTHER TONGUES, WHICH IS MY HEAVENLY LANGUAGE. THANK YOU FATHER FOR FILLING ME WITH THE HOLY SPIRIT."

Your life has totally changed, and nothing will ever be the same for you. TO GOD BE ALL THE GLORY!!! I encourage you to pray in your new heavenly language every day.